Tanya M. **Heming-Vriends**

the **Goldfish**

A guide to selection, housing,

care, nutrition, behaviour, health,

breeding and species

Contents

Contents

Foreword

Goldfish are among the most popular pets in this country, but sadly they're also one of the most neglected. Once the early enthusiasm has waned, they get scant attention, are fed a little dried food now and again and are forgotten until the next time, or until the day a poor fish drifts belly-up on the surface. The reason behind this misery is that most people don't know exactly how goldfish should be kept and cared for, despite the fact that goldfish can make fascinating pets and, with proper care, can live for many years.

Instead of buying a fish and fishbowl on impulse, we recommend you first find out what you need to know to really enjoy this fascinating hobby. Once you know what and why, you will discover that there are many aspects to keeping and breeding goldfish, and you will automatically derive more pleasure from it. Furthermore, your goldfish will be better for it and not give up the ghost after just a few weeks. This small book will put you on the right track. It will show you that a hobby begun well can be full of happy moments.

Tanya M. Heming-Vriends was born in the Hague, the Netherlands, but moved as a child with her parents to the United States. After high school, she studied art history, biology and business studies at the University of Cincinnati, Ohio. After earning her degree, she worked for a well-known American publisher in New York. Together with her father, the renowned biologist and aviculturalist Professor Dr. Thijs Vriends, she has published various biology and animal books.

About Pets

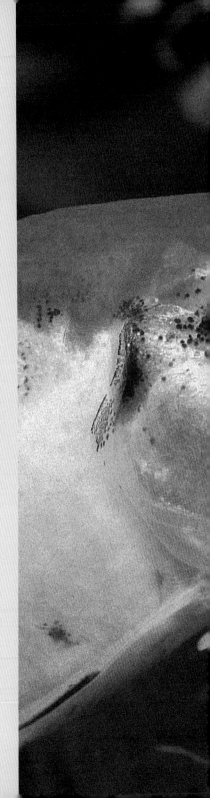

about pets

A Publication of About Pets.

Copyright © 2003
About Pets
co-publisher United Kingdom
Kingdom Books
PO9 5TL, England

ISBN 185279223X
First printing
September 2003
Second printing
May 2004

Original title: *de Goudvis*
© 2002 Welzo Media Productions bv,
About Pets bv,
Warffum, the Netherlands
www.aboutpets.info

Photos:
Rob Doolaard, Frans Maas,
Rob Dekker, Velda products
Drawings:
Diseases: Aquamor
Equiment: Tanya M. Heming-Vriends

Illustrations: Tanya M. Heming-Vriends
Editor: Karen Wolters

Printed in China

In general

The goldfish is a fish that is not naturally found in the wild. It is generally accepted that the goldfish *(Carassius auratus)* is the domesticated form of the copper-coloured crucian or gibel carp *(Carassius auratus gibelio).*

Comet fish

This carp often displays golden-red colour variations that breeders over the centuries have selectively bred and genetically transformed into the goldfish. The copper-coloured crucian carp is normally green or brown in colour, but some individuals displayed a golden-red colour and were selected for breeding goldfish.

Origins

The goldfish is an ancient species. Various documents confirm that breeders in China were already working on this variety in 960 AD. They named the fish 'Chin-yij'. Scarcely 200 years later, this fish was a popular pet among the nobility. In or around 1173, it was to be found in various varieties in many places. Of course, glass aquariums were not yet available

and the fish were often kept in porcelain or earthenware bowls. Outdoors, they could be admired in ornamental ponds.

Around 1500, the goldfish was also to be found as a pet in Japan. Here, this small fish was given the name 'Kingyo'. The first goldfish only arrived in Europe two centuries later. The first examples arrived in England in 1692 when a sea-captain brought the fish from Macao (China). Thirty years later the goldfish also arrived in Holland. They were imported from Java (Indonesia) from 1728 onwards. The Dutch quickly realised that there was money to be made from this variety of fish, and there were soon a large number of very efficient breeders in Holland. They played a major role in the spread of these fish throughout Europe. In the years after 1750, the goldfish found many enthusiasts in France. Germany was not far behind, and some thirty years later, there was a busy trade in goldfish there too. But they weren't cheap pets, and they were used as a status symbol by nobility and wealthy merchants. Prince Griorgi Aleksandrovich Potemkin (1739-1791), an army officer and an important figure during the years of Catherine the Great, is known to have had various goldfish in the ponds of his winter garden.

Goldfish come in so many shapes and sizes these days that one can classify them according to their accommodation needs. The first are those goldfish that can be regarded as cold-water fish. These include the larger varieties that you can buy in garden centres and keep in a pond, such as the Shubunkin and the 'normal' goldfish.
The second group is those specially bred varieties you find in pet shops. These types of goldfish are more demanding in terms of accommodation. This book primarily covers the latter group. These goldfish need an aquarium with all the necessary equipment.

Fish or miniature?
When you think about goldfish, you probably see a small gold-coloured fish in your mind.

However, in good conditions these little fish can grow to become examples of a good nine pounds. The fish we keep in aquariums, of course, can't grow to that size, and ornamental fish in the garden pond don't usually get so big and heavy either.

Appearance
Some fish experts divide the goldfish into two types: the clearly scaled goldfish and the 'unscaled' goldfish. The latter also have scales of course, but they are transparent and difficult to distinguish. The body form of the goldfish matches that of an average small carp, but the goldfish doesn't grow as broad. The goldfish is also laterally less flat and clearly rounder in form.

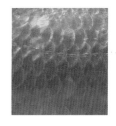

The scaly varieties are at first as good as colourless, and seem a little silvery. Only as they grow, do they first become black, and then the colours red and/or white appear.
The unscaled varieties don't possess the metallic gloss of the scaly type. We sometimes even see subtle colourings of blue, lavender or similar. The young fish are initially white with black spots, and quickly get their final colouring. A splendid unscaled variety is the Shubunkin, which originated in Japan. This fish is blue with red, yellow or red and dark brown, or a combination of these colours.

Sarasa

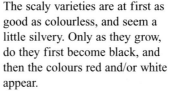

Feeding in the wild

Although the goldfish is a variety bred by man, this fish is now often found in the wild. These are examples that have been put out in the wild, and now are often found in their thousands in the waters around the Mediterranean Sea. The fish has also been observed in sub-tropical America. These 'wildened' goldfish live in both flowing and still waters and they live on both animal and vegetable food.

Sarasa

Their animal food consists of fleas, freshwater shrimps, mosquito larvae and worms (including primarily tubifex) while their vegetable food consists of duckweed, algae and young water plants. Goldfish will also fill their mouths with mud from the bottom, chew on it for a while and finally spit the sand and other residue out. They will have filtered out any pieces of plant or animal remains and eaten them. How they actually do this is not yet precisely known.

A closer look at the goldfish: Ichthyology

Ichthyology is the study of fish. The body temperature of a fish is dependent on its environment; they breathe through gills and their skin is covered in bony scales. They also have fins and reproduce by means of eggs without shells. Their body shape is totally adapted to living in water. If you hold a goldfish in your hand it will feel totally slippery because it has no cuticle layer. The smooth mucous layer makes mobility in water easier, and this layer is continuously topped up by glands in the skin. The bony scales (consisting of bony tissue, as the name implies) are formed within the leathery skin and lay on it superimposed like roof tiles.

Movement

The fish's torpedo-shaped body eases movement through water; the transition from head to rump is generally very gradual. Its movement is twisting from side to side, in a wave from head to tail. The pectoral and pelvic fins are used as brakes or for turns and for 'standing' in water. The well-developed tail fin (or caudal fin) is actually of secondary importance for movement. All fins consist of bony rays which are connected by a membrane.

Breathing

Goldfish breathe through the red gills that are easily visible by lifting the gill cover. A gill is built of thin folds of skin which are arranged in a double row along the gill arch. When breathing, the water flows in through the mouth, then through the elaborate gill filaments, along the gills and out again through the gill cover. There are also so-called 'lungfish'. These fish use their gills in water. When on land, the air bladder takes in swallowed oxygen.

Blood circulation

The heart lays behind the gills and consists of one ventricle and one auricle. A ventral aorta, known as the gill aorta, extends from the ventricle with branches into the gills. The blood fed here is extremely low in oxygen. In the gills, the blood takes in oxygen which is fed into the veins that then reunite into an aorta. This aorta has branches which take oxygen to all the body organs and yield carbon dioxide to the blood. Oxygen-poor and carbon dioxide-rich blood flows through the veins to the auricle and then again into the ventricle where it is pumped through again. The goldfish thus has a very simple circulatory system.

Digestion

When humans take in food, the digestion process begins in the mouth. This is not the case with fish: the mouth sieves the food out of the water. There are tiny teeth on the gill arches, so-called plankton filters, which stop the food particles. We call that a 'gill sieve'. The short gullet steers the food towards the stomach, where the digestive process starts. From the stomach, the food enters the intestine where the pancreas and

Veiltail 'red'

Koi

Veiltail lionhead
pearl scaled

gall-bladder join. Fish have a large liver to form gall. The intestine and kidneys each have a separate outlet, so fish (except sharks) do not have a cloaca as such.

The air-bladder

The air-bladder lies between the liver and the kidney and is usually connected with the gullet. However this connection doesn't exist in some fish such as bass, sticklebacks and cod. Sharks, rays and flatfish have no air-bladder at all. The air-bladder is full of gasses which have a totally different pressure and composition to that of normal air. These gasses practically match those gasses that have an external effect on the fish. Using the connection tube with the gullet, or by means of the blood (the air-bladder wall contains a network of fine capillaries), fish can pass gasses to the air-bladder, but also pump gas out of it, for example oxygen, if the blood needs it. As a fish passes gas to the air-bladder, its specific gravity drops, causing it to rise. If gas flows out or passes into the blood, the opposite happens and the fish sinks. We call this organ a 'hydrostatic' organ. Researchers have performed many experiments with fish in this

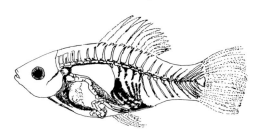

area. For example, they weighed a fish down by attaching tiny weights to it. The result was that the quantity of gas in the air-bladder increased. As the researchers made the fish lighter by tying corks to it, the gas quantity reduced.

Nervous system

The nervous system is formed by the cerebral and spinal marrow and the nerves that branch out from them. Fish have no eyelids and can only move their eyes to a very limited extent. They can distinguish between colours. Their highly sensitive scent organs are in two grooves on their head, but are not connected with their mouth. Their sense of taste is in the mouth and very probably in the whiskers that many fish possess. Water movements are sensed by the so-called lateral line that runs along the side of the fish. This is a system consisting of a large channel and a network of many tiny side-channels with sensory cells containing jelly-like protuberances. We find cells with such protuberances on the skin too. They are pressed aside by flowing water and then stimulate the sensory cells.

Hearing

Fish have an elaborate ear, which is usually connected with the air-bladder. There are fish varieties that don't have this connection and they have substantially poorer hearing. There is no cochlea present as there is in the human ear.

Pearl scaled

Feeding your goldfish

Of course, you need to know how best to feed your fish.

Sarasa

Water layers and feeding

Just as in their natural enviroment the fish in our aquaria live in certain "layers" of water. This has a major influence on their eating habits. Those that live at the bottom gather their food from the ground. This may be worms or larvae. Fish in the middle layers of the water live on insects such as midges and mosquitoes, on larvae or crustaceans such as water fleas. Surface feeders live on insects that live on the surface or land on it.

How much food?

Some fish can literally eat themselves to death, so never give too much food. There is often enough food in the aquarium itself. This may be eggs laid by one type of fish that are a real treat for others.

Cardinal Tetras are known to be egg eaters. Guppies, Black Mollys and other fish like to eat algae.

Although it depends on the fish in your aquarium, there is a rule of thumb you can follow. Feed your fish with pauses of at least two days and make sure you feed only small portions so that nothing falls to the bottom where it might rot.

Types of food

There are three types of food you might use if you want to keep a flourishing aquarium with happy fish. There is live food consisting of tiny living animals such as mosquito larvae and water fleas. You can buy frozen food in the pet shop and there is the well-known dry food.

Live food

You can often buy live food in good aquarium shops. There are some aquarium lovers that catch their live food themselves in ditches and ponds. If you decide to do that remember to use a white bucket in which you can see precisely what you've caught and prevent introducing unwanted guests into your aquarium. The following are a few examples of live food. Very popular are water fleas and so-called copepoda. There are also various types of mosquito and midge larvae. Red midge larvae are larvae of the "dancing midge" *(Chironomus plumosus)*. You might encounter white midge larvae when catching water fleas. These are the larvae of a midge that doesn't bite and you can recognise it by its transparent body. The white midge larvae can be bought in aquarium shops in tubes filled with water and larvae. The larvae can be kept for quite a while in the tube without food or oxygen. Be careful with black midge larvae, which are those of the biting midge. Don't bring too many into your house or you'll wind up with an infestation of midges.

Frozen food

Almost all live foods can also be bought in frozen form. As a beginner, these may be your best choice to avoid introducing irregularities into your aquarium.

However, there is one major disadvantage in frozen foods. They don't encourage your fish to hunt, although that is part of their nature.

Dry food

Dry food is available in all shapes and sizes. The disadvantage of dry food is that most drift on the surface. Some fish gobble the food up at the surface and take in so much air that this gets into their intestines and can kill them. You can prevent this by soaking the food before you sprinkle it in your aquarium.

Dry food

A home for your goldfish

You can keep goldfish in various ways, but one home is not the same as another and it is important to give your goldfish a proper place to live.

Veiltail 'redcap'

In this section, we discuss the advantages and disadvantages of two forms of home. You will learn what requirements goldfish have in terms of their living environment.

The pro's and con's of a fishbowl

The advantages of a fishbowl are of benefit only to the fish-owner. The fish, of course, would benefit from much more space to live in, but most fishbowls aren't large enough. You can place a fishbowl practically anywhere, but not every place is suitable. In front of a window in the full sun, for example, is a poor place. An advantage of a fishbowl is that you can move it around easily, and it's a simple job to keep it clean. A disadvantage is that there is room for two small fish at most.

Most fishbowls hold some four litres of water and that's really only just enough for one fish.

Water surface

But it's not the size of the bowl and the amount of water it can hold that is most important for your goldfish. They would benefit more from having enough surface area. A goldfish breathes by taking in oxygen from the water, and it also gives off carbondioxide into the water. This always happens close to the surface. If the surface area is too small, the water absorbs too little oxygen and can not give off enough carbondioxide. Your fish will die. There are fishbowls in the shops with a very narrow neck. If you fill this to the top with water thinking you're doing your fish a favour, then there's a good chance that your fish won't be able to get enough oxygen. Fill the bowl only halfway with water and the surface is then usually much larger.

Furniture

A fishbowl must be equipped just like an aquarium so that it's comfortable for its resident(s). There is a huge assortment of undergravels, hideaways and plants available. You can choose gravel in many colours, rocks, filters and even plastic plants.

Housekeeping

It's easy to forget to clean a fishbowl, but it is very important. Because of the relatively small dimensions, the water can get dirtier much quicker than in an aquarium. When you clean your fishbowl, you must temporarily put the fish in a bucket or a tank

with water. Then you can put in fresh water, clean the sand, gravel and rocks properly and, if you use a filter, you must also clean that. Don't forget to check the filter for any faults. A fishbowl should be cleaned once a week. The fresh water should be at approximately the same temperature as the fish are used to swimming in. Many a goldfish has suddenly gone to the great fishpond in the sky after a sudden dive into cold water. The animal can go into shock.

Pro's and con's of an aquarium

Fish will enjoy life in an aquarium **far more** than in a fishbowl because of the extra space. And with an aquarium, you can create a beautiful natural backdrop in your own home. The only things you need are the aquarium itself, some rocks, sand or gravel, wall covering and plants. You can get

years of pleasure from an aquarium. There are various models available in shops, and you can choose glass or polyester containers. A disadvantage of an aquarium is that it is somewhat more expensive, especially compared to a fishbowl, but you may be able to get over that hurdle by looking for a good second-hand aquarium.

A place for an aquarium

From now on, we're talking about an aquarium, but by far the most points we cover in this small book also apply to goldfish kept in a fishbowl. Before filling an aquarium, you need to think about where it is to stand. Once an aquarium is equipped, it's not easy to move, if only because of the

weight. The choice of location will depend largely on the size and shape of your aquarium, and you also need to consider the table or cupboard you're going to put your aquarium on. This needs to be strong enough to carry the weight. If that's not the case there's a risk that the cupboard, shelf or whatever else your aquarium stands on will sag. Your aquarium is then not getting even support and may crack. The room's floor must also be strong enough to hold the weight. With concrete floors this will not be an issue, but wooden floors might pose a problem.

If you do decide you're strong enough to move a full aquarium remember the following. Because of the weight and pressure of the water, panels may break or crack. On a frame aquarium, the seams or joints may start to leak. Finally, if you slosh the water around too much, your fish may go into shock. There are other points you need to consider when placing your aquarium. There must be electricity sockets nearby for filter and light connections. Hide cables behind the aquarium so that nobody can trip over them. Make sure you can get at the aquarium easily to clean it or to feed your fish. Try not to put it close to a door. The vibrations caused by the opening and closing of a door can be disastrous for your fish, and if you own a cat, you need to keep an eye on that too…

Veiltail 'Calico'

Light

Your aquarium must never stand in the full sun, but light is also very important. Algae can form if there's too little light getting into the aquarium, and the plants in the aquarium won't flourish either. If you do want to locate your aquarium close to a window, choose a window facing east. In the winter, you certainly won't have enough sunlight and you'll have to add some light. Most aquariums are fitted with a light hood as standard.

Too much direct sunlight can cause the water temperature to rise, and you need to be careful here. A temperature higher than 24°C will feel very uncomfortable for your goldfish, mainly because the quantity of oxygen drops quickly in warmer water. This can have fatal consequences in an aquarium with several fish. (Gold)fish can't handle temperature fluctuations well, so never put an aquarium in a draughty location or anywhere close to heaters or air-conditioners.

Aquarium types

Most aquariums are made of glass or Perspex and are frameless. This means that the seams are "unbreakable". Many all-glass aquariums do have a top edging, but this is always for purely decorative purposes. There are also plastic aquariums on sale but these are not advisable. They are often small, break quickly and are very vulnerable to scratches. If you're serious about your hobby, buy a glass aquarium. The shape is also important. A square container with a large surface area is better for your goldfish than a tall model with a smaller water surface.

Veiltail 'red'

Dimensions

Before you buy an aquarium, you must know exactly what you want to do with it. 'Keeping fish' is not enough information. Firstly, make sure you have enough room for the model you want to buy.

Secondly, you need to think about the number of (gold)fish you plan to keep. Goldfish like plenty of room. You can use the following rule of thumb: for each litre of water there is room for one fish three centimetres in length. If your goldfish is nine centimetres long, it needs three litres of water. Also think about the life expectancy of a fish of course.

Young goldfish are still small but, of course, they'll grow, so stick to three litres of water for these fish too. Goldfish are sturdy in form (flat and wide) and the bigger and sturdier the fish, the more oxygen it needs. Also take into account the fact that goldfish will grow 'with' their container. If you give goldfish the freedom of a big aquarium, they will grow very fast. So it's good advice to have an aquarium of at least 60 litres for five goldfish.

Things you need for an aquarium

A good home for goldfish is more than just an aquarium tank. There are other things you need for a water eco-system to function properly.

Veiltail 'red'

In this section you can learn what apparatus and other equipment you need to buy to get maximum pleasure from your aquarium.

Cover panel
Your goldfish won't deliberately jump out of your aquarium, but this is not totally unheard of. If goldfish are seriously frightened, or if the water is dirty and poor in oxygen, they can certainly jump 10 centimetres out of the water. A fish may also jump out of the water if it's bothered by parasites or other pests that have attached themselves to its gills. So you need to make sure that the aquarium is equipped with a cover panel. Cover panels don't only stop fish jumping out of an aquarium, but they also prevent unwanted substances getting into

the water, and they also help prevent too much evaporation. You will certainly notice that droplets of condensation gather on the underside of the cover panel. These mostly drop back into the water and can help cool it down. This can be very useful on warm summer days.

In aquariums with cover panels the water thus stays in longer and that's good news. After all, the more water the more oxygen. Furthermore, more water can handle more droppings and other pollutants.

Light hoods
If you want artificial light in your aquarium then a light hood is the best choice. You then don't need a cover panel. Light hoods often

work on low voltage, which means you'll need a transformer.

Try to maintain a normal day/night rhythm with the lighting, meaning approximately 12 hours of darkness and 12 hours of light. This will keep algae growth under control and plants will flourish - they react positively to light. During the day, plants breathe oxygen in, and during the night they give it off again. This is an important process for your aquarium. If the lighting is on 20 hours per day then the plants will only breathe oxygen in. The time they have to give oxygen off is too short and over time your plants will wane. Not only is the lighting time (number of hours) and the colour of your lighting (some plants need green or red lamps) important, but also the wattage. When buying your aquarium, ask what wattage is required for the light hood that goes with it. There are light hoods that you can put light bulbs in, but a small neon tube is better. A light hood with neon tubes gives off a softer and more natural light and is less costly in consumption. They also give off less heat, reducing the chance of condensation.

Heating elements

Goldfish are cold-water fish, and water at a temperature of 18 - 20°C is excellent for them. There are also goldfish varieties that can stand lower water temperatures if they have to, so a heating element is not really a necessity.

Young Shubunkin

However, winter weather may mean you need one, especially if you have a small aquarium and live in a house with no central heating. In an aquarium with 20 - 40 litres, the water temperature can drop from 21°C to 4 - 10°C within a few hours. Goldfish can go into shock in water that cold, and will often die or become seriously ill. If you have a heating element, set it at 18°C. Then if the water temperature does drop, it won't bother your fish.

If you're not sure what sort of heating element you need for your aquarium, or you want to be sure the element that was supplied with your aquarium is the right one,

Top: Shubunkin
Bottom: Sarasa

use the following rule of thumb: You need 0.6 - 1.2 watts for each litre of water. If you have a 40 litre tank, buy a heating element of 25 - 50 watts. There are also elements available with a built-in thermostat. These elements sense water temperature fluctuations and switch on as soon as it's necessary. However, these elements do have one small disadvantage; they don't show the actual water temperature. You still need to measure the temperature with the help of a thermometer.

Thermometers
If you want to be serious about your hobby, you must check the water temperature daily with one

or two thermometers. There are two types of thermometer. One works with an alcohol mixture coloured red. These thermometers are fixed in the aquarium with red suction feet. The other type are attached to the outside wall of the tank with a rubber suction pad. There are also digital thermometers in the shops that you can attach to the outside of your aquarium. Take care when placing thermometers in the water. If they are too close to a heat source they may give a false reading, and you don't want fish colliding with the thermometer at full speed.

Filters

Various types of filter are available from pet shops. Most are made as follows: a layer of fibre-glass, then a layer of active carbon, then another layer of fibre-glass and finally a layer of coarse gravel (the latter prevents the filter becoming blocked). Fibre-glass stops fine particles, and active carbon purifies the water. It will also eliminate any smells and ensure a practically constant acidity in the water. Most models are nothing more than an extractor, a combination of two tubes of different diameters. By blowing air through the tube that is fitted below the wide pipe, air bubbles rise to the surface drawing the water with them. This causes a suction effect in the filter chamber.

You can choose between the following types of filter. If you're not sure what type you need, ask for information in a specialist aquarium shop or from your local aquarium association.

1. The horizontal internal filter (attached inside the aquarium, directly on top of the sand); this type is the easiest to hide among the fittings in the aquarium (for example behind driftwood (fossilised wood), a rock or a group of plants etc.). A disadvantage is poor performance because the water stream is horizontal.

2. The vertical internal filter (this is also laid on the sand and can be 'hidden'). Performance is better than that of the horizontal filter.

3. The vertical external filter. This is perhaps the most efficient type for a goldfish aquarium, despite the fact that it takes more space than the other two types. The filter 'sits' in a metal frame and is attached to the outside of the aquarium. The water enters via a siphon (which hangs in the water inside the aquarium) and exits via a cellulose or plastic tube. This is a fast form of filtering.

Air pump

The air pump actually has a dual purpose: firstly, it delivers the energy for the filter to do its work and it serves to pump fresh air into the aquarium. The pump produces compressed air that is delivered to the filter siphon.

Thermometer

Filter

a magnet to
clean the glass

You can regulate the intake level yourself with a valve; if you put a branch into the pipe you can deliver air to a second point with an aerator stone creating excellent water circulation. You can leave the pump working 24 hours per day, but make sure it is placed a little higher than the water level to prevent any overflowing. Of course, the air sucked in by the air pump must be clean. If people smoke in the room, the air is going to be impure.

Fish-net

You can buy all kinds of fish-nets, small or large, in your aquarium shop. You may need to take fish out of the aquarium, so make sure the net can be manoeuvred freely in the water. Use a net which is not too small in cross-section. If you have a 40 litre tank, a net of 15 - 18 cm cross-section is ideal. Remember that goldfish can jump up once they're lifted up in the net, so cover the net with your thumb and index finger before lifting it out of the water. Don't forget to put the net in boiling water for 25 seconds or so before use to ensure it is free of any parasites or other 'nasties' that may have gathered in it when it was laying dry in the cupboard since it was last used.

Aquarium cleaners

You can clean the inside of your aquarium with a scraper with felt or with a scraper with a blade. Only use a blade if algae have really stuck fast on the pane and try to avoid scratching the glass. You can also use magnets to clean the glass. One magnet on the outside and another inside the tank moved vertically up and down will wipe the algae from the glass. By the way, goldfish like to eat algae so you won't need to clean too much.

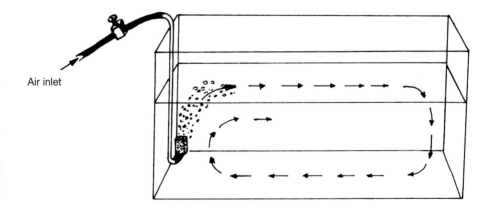

Air inlet

Cleaning the floor

Fish droppings and dead leaves from the water plants on the floor of the aquarium must be removed from time to time. If not, there's a risk that the water will become contaminated and poor in oxygen. The best tool is a small glass or plastic siphon. A rubber hose can be used for larger aquariums, with a glass or plastic tube at the end with which you can 'sweep' the floor. It works like a vacuum cleaner. Once you've applied suction to the tube, the water will start to flow. Let the water into a bucket, and then filter it through a thick cotton cloth before putting the old water back into the aquarium.

Vacuum cleaner for your aquarium

Caring for an aquarium

The phrase 'prevention is better than a cure' certainly applies to your aquarium. If everything in your aquarium is in order, your fish won't get sick and your plants won't die. This means you need good quality heating, ventilation and filter systems. Penny-wise is, sadly, often pound-foolish.

Make it a habit to take a quick look at the thermometer whenever you're in the proximity of your aquarium, and check the ventilation system daily. It only needs a few moments and can prevent a lot of heartache. Aerator stones can quickly get blocked by algae and salt deposits causing back-pressure on the pump. Eventually the diaphragm will start to leak. Also check the filter once a week. The water and air tubes can get blocked by algae or slimy dirt. This also applies to the fibre-glass and carbon. A blockage means poor water and air throughput, or none at all. Replace the fibre-glass and carbon regularly. Leave a few shreds of the old fibre-glass and two teaspoonfuls of the old carbon in the filter. This activates the biological filtering process. If you don't do this, the aquarium water will stay turbid for a few days. If you've hidden your filter under the gravel, very carefully lift it out and then push it back in once in a while. This will prevent the filter becoming blocked. Be sure to clean the gravel once in a while with a small vacuum cleaner.

Veiltail 'red-white'

A lot of dirt can get into the gravel, be it old food remnants, droppings etc. If you don't keep it clean, it will become a breeding ground for bacteria and moulds.

Fish and stress
It is well known that stress can attack a fish's immune system, making it more vulnerable to disease and parasites. Stress among fish can be caused by having too many fish in the tank, dirty water, too much vibration close to the aquarium or due to change. Parasites, bacteria, viruses and mould lay waiting to attack an over-stressed fish. A fish suffering from stress gradually loses the mucous layer on its skin. Without this layer the fish is inevitably exposed to disease. You should do everything you can to ensure your fish don't suffer from stress.

The aquarium water
Opinions differ widely on refreshing aquarium water. Some aquarium lovers say you should replace one fifth of the water each week, others say a third. The author of this book has another opinion. If you keep your aquarium in perfect condition, you only need to replace the water after five years. This means your

Young Golden Orfe. This species can grow up to 50-80 cm and is therefore only suitable for a bigger garden pond

equipment must be in perfect working order and that you remove any dead fish or (parts of) plants from the water immediately. However, you do need to top the water up regularly. Some water will evaporate after all, especially due to the heating and lighting. As long as you don't need to top up half of the aquarium, but just two litres or so for a 40 litre tank, then you don't need to worry about the water chemistry.

The following is a good rule: If you have a 40 litre tank, replace one litre of water each week. Add a little more to compensate for evaporation. In this way, no major chemical changes will happen as you refresh the water. Apart from that, you can use normal tapwater, because all the chemical elements needed are in the aquarium already and tap water will not endanger your fish.

Water contamination

One of the main contaminants in aquarium water is excess goldfish food. Feeding goldfish properly is a real art, regardless of whether you feed food in flakes, in frozen form or live food. The golden rule is: always feed in driblets, whatever type of food you use. Your fish must have eaten it all within five minutes (although fish eating always looks like they are wolfing it down). Goldfish have no table manners, and they'll keep scoffing food down if they get the chance. They will eat as long as it takes for them to become so heavy that they slowly sink to the bottom of the aquarium and wait there until the food is digested. Fish that eat a lot also leave a lot of droppings in the water, making life hard work for your filter, so you need to be sure that your filter is up to the job. As far as feeding times are concerned follow the rule: fully grown fish once per day, preferably in the morning; young, growing fish twice a day (mornings and late afternoon); older fish (four years and older) once every two days.

Veiltail 'Calico'

Plants in an aquarium

An aquarium with only fish in it is not natural. Water plants and fish together can make an aquarium like a piece of living nature. However, you do need to be careful what sorts of fish and plants you choose, and whether they suit each other.

Cognac Plant
*(Ammania
senegalensis)*

Why plants are so important
Under the influence of light, plants generate oxygen, and the goldfish in your aquarium badly need that oxygen. So they can't live without plants. Goldfish also like to nibble at plants and to hide amongst them from time to time. Goldfish will hide themselves if it's busy around the aquarium or there's something causing agitation in the tank.

Plastic plants or living plants?
Plants in a newly equipped aquarium often have a tough time for the first six months or so. This is because the water and bed have not been able to build up enough nutrients. If you choose plants that have too little reserves of nutrients, they may even die. Some people therefore choose

plastic plants. There's no bother with dead plants and they always look nice. Your fish can still hide away and they can't eat the plants away. Goldfish are omnivorous and will eat both animal and vegetable food. Young plants and sprouting leaves are sometimes too much of a temptation. They will also nibble at plastic plants, but you don't need to worry about that. They do this looking for algae and micro-organisms which they eat off the plastic leaves.

If you're a little more persevering, use real plants. These grow and multiply and some bloom with beautiful tiny flowers. You can also put some plastic plants among the real ones, of course. Then you're always sure to have a fine green background.

Living plants

Because goldfish simply will not leave living plants alone, it's important to choose plants with a strong rootstock (from the rootstock grow the roots and stems): *Aponogeton* and some *Cryptocoryne* and *Echinodorus* varieties are excellent examples here. Plants such as the *Vallisneria*, most *Sagittaria*, *Hygrophila* and *Myriophyllum* varieties don't have a rootstock and are hardly likely to survive in an aquarium without nutrient reserves.

Most of the living plants you can buy in an aquarium shop are intended for tropical aquariums. However, you need plants that can survive in cold water at the same temperature as your goldfish (18 - 21°C). Some plants grow better in acid water, or in water with a low pH value. Your goldfish don't like acid water, so these plants are best left out of your aquarium.

As far as plants are concerned, stick to the following rules:
1. Most plants thrive well in very alkaline water with a pH over 8.
2. Plants also do well in slightly acid water with a pH of 6.8.
3. Water plants develop well in neutral water: pH 7.0.
4. The same applies to soft alkaline water pH 7.2 to 7.6 (tap-water).

Plant lighting

If plants don't get light, they die. Natural sunlight is important for healthy growth and oxygen generation. Unfortunately the sun doesn't shine exactly 12 hours per day and this means you need to supplement it with artificial light. See chapter 1 for more information on lighting.

Location and underfloor

The floor of your aquarium is the feeding ground for the plants. You can cover the floor with turf from specialist aquarium shops. Two centimetres is often enough. Over that you can lay a three centimetre thick layer of gravel. This gives the plants a good chance of not being pulled out by avaricious goldfish. If you're worried about that, you can lay a heavy stone approximately over the spot where the roots are. This will give them extra protection. To give your aquarium more depth (which makes it look larger), put plants that only grow low towards the front and high growers in the rear corners and against the back panel. You can disguise your heating element(s) and ventilation pumps behind the high growing plants. It may be useful to take a look at an especially attractive aquarium to see how it has been arranged. This can give you a lot of inspiration.

Plants for the aquarium

There are many plants suitable for your aquarium. In this chapter, we'll cover a number of plants that are excellent for goldfish tanks.

Giant Bacoba
(Bacopa carolineana)

Red Cabomba
(Cabomba furcata)

*Alternathera
reineckii sessilis*

Indian Fern or Sumatra Fern (Ceratopteris thalicroides)

This light green plant also comes as a drifting plant. It forms spurs on its leaves that stick out of the water. As the plant gets bigger it takes on the form of a fern. It multiplies from the roots and by offshoots. It is easy to keep, grows best in normal, slightly acid (pH 5 - 6.5) aquarium water at a temperature between 21 and 27°C. Its fragile, finely distributed leaves have to put up with a lot, but even small parts of a leaf can develop new leaf buds. The 'foot'

The pH value represents the acidity level of the water, or more precisely: the concentration of oxygen ions. This is measured on a scale from 1 to 14. The acidity level has even more influence on our fish than the water hardness itself. pH stands for 'pondus hydrogenii', which means the weight of the oxygen, i.e. the weight of all oxygen ions in one litre of water. Water with a pH value of 7.0 is neutral, and this pH level is important for almost all fish.

If the pH value climbs above 7, then the water is alkaline, if it goes under 7 then the water is acid. pH levels above 9 and under 5 are fatal for water residents. There are liquid indicators available in specialist shops. There are also test papers and tablets, but paper indicators are the least reliable. If your water is too alkaline, you can use anorganic acids that are available in specialist shops to acidise it.

Always handle these acids with great care. If you get them on your skin you can suffer a nasty burn. Feed the acid into the water through the ventilation tube or the outlet from your filter. Check the pH value again after each dosage.

If the pH value goes under 5, you can bring it back to the right level using calcium hydroxide. However, it is a lot simpler and much more natural to soften the water, and at the same time acidise it with fibrous turf. Ask for more information at your aquarium shop or your local club. There are plenty of other methods. If the water is too acid you can dissolve a little bicarbonate in a glass of water and feed it into your aquarium water. If it's too alkaline then you need to acidise it. You can do this with primary sodium phosphate. This also needs to be dissolved first in a glass of water.

Never be too radical, and keep checking the pH. If the water is still not as it should be, then add a further dose every two days until it's at the right level again.

Petch's Waterchalice
(Cryptocoryne petchii)

of the plant must stand just a little above the ground. This splendid plant grows fast. Even goldfish seem unable to hinder its growth. The plant is found over a huge area. It appears in Africa, Southeast Asia and tropical parts of America. The best soil for this plant is normal turf.

Cryptocoryne

This plant from the tropics belongs to the arum family. To develop well it needs a lot of light and a good soil (see the Indian fern). *Cryptocoryne* varieties possess a well-developed root system. This plant, which has spear-shaped leaves about 15 centimetres long, is best placed in the foreground. It does not like temperatures below 21°C.

The *Cryptocoryne becketii* and *Cryptocoryne willisii* (previously known as *nevellii*) varieties were cultivated for trading in Europe. The former variety originally comes from Sri Lanka and is well suited for our goldfish aquarium.

Java Fern
(Microsorium pteropus)

The Java Fern is a plant with a strong rootstock. Its leaves are long, in light and dark green and stand out beautifully against a dark background. In cold water, its leaves never get longer than about 10 centimetres; in tropical aquariums they can grow to some 25 centimetres. The roots can attach themselves to gravel, rocks or a piece of driftwood. This plant originated in India and Southern

Brazilian Pennyword
(Hydrocotyle leuco-
cephala)

Crinkled Apenogeton
(Apenogeton crispus)

China and wide regions of Asia to the Philippines. It will grow even in poor light and can withstand acid or alkaline water. The temperature must be between 21 and 25°C. Put a heavy stone over the part of the ground where the rootstock is, so that the fish can't pull it free. If you use driftwood, you can carefully attach the plant to it with thin fishing line (available in fishing tackle shops). The Java Fern's roots will eventually attach themselves firmly into the wood.

Aponogeton varieties

There are some 45 known varieties of *Aponogeton*. The majority of these well-known and strong growing plants come from the tropical regions of Asia.

The strongest varieties are *Aponogeton crispus*, *Aponogeton undulatus*, and *Aponogeton natans*. From Australia comes the *Aponogeton elongatus*. All varieties need a temperature between 21 and 28°C and water hardness of 60 – 80 mg/l. They are best kept in larger aquariums (40 litres or more). They go through a rest period from November until approximately January and then lose almost all their leaves. It can be useful to take the bulb-shaped rootstock out of the ground and lay it in the aquarium water, or keep it in a separate tank until it develops new leaves. Then you can set the rootstock back into the ground. The stems of *Aponogeton undulatus* don't have flowers but

bloom with complete miniature plants at the end of its ball-shaped spikes. The flowers of *Aponogeton crispus* and *Aponogeton elongatus* are white. All these plants develop excellently in a sand and turf soil.

Sword Plants *(Echinodorus)*

There are some 50 known varieties of the Sword Plant. Good foreground plants are *Echinodorus tenellus*, *Echinodorus quadricostatus* and *Echinodorus latifolius* because they need a lot of light. Unfortunately, they don't always survive the attention of permanently hungry goldfish. *Echinodorus bleheri*, however, can be used well. Its leaves are seven to eight centimetres wide and dark

Large Cognac Plant
(Ammania gracilis)

Hard and soft water

When we talk of water hardness, we mean the amount of calcium carbonate that is dissolved in one litre of water. Too much calcium carbonate is harmful to fish, so it's important we know how hard the water is. Hardness is measured in milligrams per litre, so a hardness of 100 mg/l means that 100 milligrams of calcium carbonate are dissolved in one litre. More precisely spoken, hardness in water is caused by dissolved calcium and magnesium salts. Soft water is thus water with low dissolved calcium and magnesium salt levels. Total hardness consists of two components:

1. Calcium and magnesium compounds which, together with carbon dioxide, form so-called temporary hardness.
2. All other calcium and magnesium salts, which cause so-called permanent hardness.

Total hardness is the same as temporary hardness (also called carbonate hardness) plus permanent hardness (non-carbonate hardness). This means that the total hardness less the temporary hardness is the same as the permanent hardness.

The ideal every aquarium lover should strive for is a total hardness of 60 mg/l. Most fish can be bred in this and aquarium plants will flourish. A hardness of 0 – 30 mg/l means that the water is soft. You can buy various products for measuring the hardness of your water in aquarium shops.

There are various methods to soften water. The first is a softener filter for which you need no knowledge of chemistry. A simple way to get soft water is to mix rainwater or distilled water (can only be made with special equipment, ask your aquarium dealer) with hard water. To get the right ratio you need to know that distilled water has a hardness of 0 mg/l, but is somewhat expensive.

Crinkled Apenogeton
(Apenogeton crispus)

Cognac Plant
(Ammania
senegalensis)

Cabomba aquatica

green in colour. The flower stem stays underwater and generates new plants. Sword Plants need a normal soil, water of 60 to 80 mg/l hardness and a pH value of about 7. The temperature should be approximately 23°C. Another 'easy' plant for a small aquarium is the *Echinodorus parviflorus*. Once it's established it spreads rapidly, so don't plant it too close to other plants. Both plants need lighting that is not too strong.

Vallis varieties

Here too, many varieties are known. The best plant for a goldfish aquarium is and will stay the *Vallisneria spiralis* also known as the Straight Vallis. This plant has somewhat bluish roots and long, thin light green leaves that can grow up to 80 cm and be a good one centimetre wide. It has spirally rolled white flowers which, after unrolling, appear on the surface. Fertilisation then takes place by male flowers that stand on short stilts. The buds are located at the foot of the long leaves and are released, rise to the surface and spring open.
The root offshoots take care of multiplication. If the offshoots come out of the ground, there is too little light. If they grow deep, there is too much light. The temperature must never drop below 15°C. Origin: Southern Europe.

Myriophyllum (Water milfoil) varieties

This gender of plant is characterised by its strongly branched, vertical stems with rings and it has feather-shaped leaves with slits. If it grows above the surface of the water these slits are then substantially shorter. This plant needs lots of light, but you need to watch out for algae growth. It grows best on a sand floor with a little clay or turf.
The Parrot Feather Milfoil *(Myriophyllum brasiliense)* is excellent for a goldfish tank. Its long and slender stem is soft and curly underwater. The male flowers consist of four pink and white crown leaves. The water level must not be less than 40 cm, otherwise the plant grows out of the water. Origin: South America.

The *Myriophyllum elationoides* has feather-shaped leaves in rings of three to five standing leaves. These leaves are dark blue-green and are one to two centimetres long. This plant suits an unheated aquarium well but does need a lot of light. Origin: South America, Northern Brazil, Mexico, Tasmania, New Zealand, Falkland Islands.

Myriophyllum hippuriodes is also a slender plant with strong stems and suitable for cold- or warm-water aquariums. Its feather-shaped leaves have six to ten tails. Bi-sexual (self-fertilising) flowers often appear close to the surface;

at the top of the stem are a large number of male flowers. They need a lot of light and like a ground with some clay worked in. Origin: North America and Mexico.

The *Myriophyllum scabratum*, on the other hand, is a fine plant with a large number of forked stems. This plant grows low. Its leaves stand in rings of three, but also opposite each other or in spirals; there are often multiple rings. The plant is soft green in colour and stands some four centimetres high. It does well in cold- or warm-water aquariums and is easy to make cuttings of. The *Myriophyllum scrabratum* is actually indispensable in a breeding tank because fish like to lay their eggs on it.

Origin: The Eastern part of North America, Eastern Mexico and Cuba.

Hygrophila varieties

The *Hygrophila polysperma* or Indian Water Star is a plant with stems up to 50 centimetres long. The leaves stand opposite each other, are light green in colour and long and oval. They are some four centimetres long and one and a half centimetres wide. They can withstand temperatures up to 30°C. They need no special lighting but do much better in strong light. Each piece of stem offers the chance of offshoots at the surface. Origin: India.

Indian Water Star
(Hygrophila polysperma)

Goldfish

Setting up an aquarium

It sounds really simple: fill aquarium, put in fish and done! Unfortunately it's usually not that simple in practice. There's a lot of work to be done to develop a water eco-system that is just right. In this chapter you can read how to set up an aquarium properly.

Checking the tank

Before filling the aquarium, you need to check it for leaks. Stand it on a strong horizontal surface and fill it with water. If possible, do this outdoors as long as it's not freezing. Small leaks can be repaired with silicone sealant. If there are major leaks you need to take it back to the aquarium shop. Most aquariums are insured by the manufacturer. Inform yourself well before you buy an aquarium or any other equipment for it. Your aquarium must be totally leak-proof before you set it in its final location.

Gravel

Gravel on the bottom of the tank can be very decorative. Make sure it's gravel of good quality. Porous gravel is not recommended, because food remnants can get stuck in any openings and contaminate the water. There are all kinds of gravel for aquariums in specialist shops, even in different colours. If you want your aquarium to appear natural, don't buy coloured gravel. Before putting the gravel in your tank, wash it thoroughly in a strong stream of water.

Nutrient soil

You may want to leave the central part of your aquarium free of plants and then a floor of properly washed sharp sand or gravel is sufficient. Gravel alone, however, is not enough in places where you plan plants. There you need to create a good soil (nutrient soil) for your plants. A nutrient soil of turf and coarse sand is sufficient.

Some plants need a heavier soil, but you may consider placing these plants on the ground in pots filled with soil suitable for them.

You can buy many nutrient soils ready-made in aquarium shops, but you can also make them up yourself using well watered turf. Make sure this turf has not been chemically treated. Mix the turf with unwashed river sand (also available in specialist shops). Then put in the soil so that it creates an optical perspective. At the front of the tank it is approximately two centimetres deep and, at the back, five to eight centimetres. Decorate your aquarium with stones, driftwood and other items. It's advisable not to use more than two different types of stone. Fossilised wood must first be soaked in a bucket of water so that it doesn't float to the surface. You can then nail it to a small plank so that the fish can't knock it over later. Of course you can also make this plank of fossilised wood and cover it with the nutrient soil so that it can't be seen.

You can also build some terraces, but remember that daylight will always shine in obliquely towards the back. Symmetrical terraces often don't look attractive but, of course, it's all a question of taste.

Cover the whole floor with a two centimetre layer of well washed

First fill the tank with a layer of washed sharp sand or gravel. Then add a nutrient soil for the plants. Secure the nutrient soil with another layer of washed sharp sand or gravel.

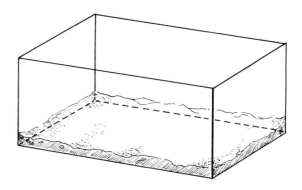

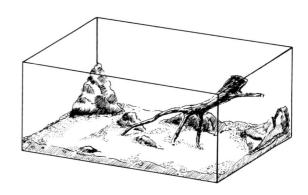

Decorate your fish tank with rocks and fossilized wood and create some terraces.

Filling of the aquarium
with water

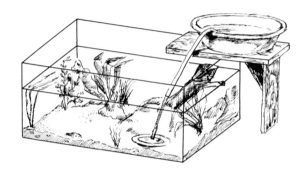

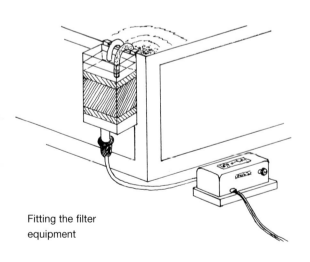

Fitting the filter
equipment

sharp sand or gravel. If you're
using a ground filter this must
naturally lie under the nutrient soil.

Pieces of rock

Rocks are not necessary of course,
but they can be ideal decoration
for your aquarium. Pieces of rock
just laid here and there have no
particular function. A better choice
is to arrange them in rows above
each other (ledges) along the
length of the aquarium. If you
create some height differences
too, this looks particularly attractive.
On the terraces you've created
you can now put a nutrient soil
and washed sand so that plants
can grow here too. Then cover the
sand with a three-centimetre layer
of gravel, otherwise your goldfish
will find a way to uproot and
nibble the plants to death.

Filling your aquarium

Once your aquarium is in the right
spot and is fully equipped except
for plants and fish, you can now
fill the tank with water. Use cold
tapwater; it does not need to be
heated and should run for a few
minutes before letting it into the
aquarium, especially if you live in
a house with copper pipes. Copper
salts are highly poisonous for fish.

On the illustration Filling (above
left) you can see how to run the
water into the aquarium. You can
also use a hose-pipe attached to
the tap. Run the water in slowly
over a board or stiff grease-free

paper to prevent the floor covering being whipped up. You can also lay a plastic refuse bag on the floor and take it out once the water is still. Only start planting once the tank is three-quarters filled with water. With the water at this level, you can easily work and you can quickly see how this and that will look when the aquarium is totally full. Always plant from front to back.

Fitting the heating element and thermostat

You might want to fit the heating and thermostat before you start planting. The advantage is that the water temperature will be more pleasant to work in while you're planting. Furthermore, any excess chlorine will disappear and that is important. Make sure that the heating element and thermostat are at least one quarter underwater. Before you start planting, leave the water to stand for several hours. Then it will be nice and clear. Switch the heating off before you start planting and check that the temperature is around 20°C.

Planting

If your tank is very deep, use planting sticks when planting. These are also helpful for areas that are difficult to reach (such as those rock ledges). Planting sticks are very useful, particularly because you don't need to disturb the plants that have already been placed. When using a planting

stick, you drive the roots into the sand after winding them around the teeth of the planting stick. A disadvantage of planting sticks is that you run a higher risk of damaging the plant's roots. If you want to plant by hand, proceed as follows:

Hold the roots and the foot of the plant between your outstretched thumb and first two fingers. Turn the longer roots round your index finger. Now press straight into the sand until deep into the nutrient soil. The fingers make the hole while the roots are protected. Now stretch your thumb and press the roots into the sand with your index finger. Your thumb and middle finger hold the green part of the plant. Then check the position of the plant. If it's properly lined up then close the hole with your hand. Make sure the foot of the plant is above the gravel, otherwise it will rot away.

After planting

When all the plants have been placed, you can now fill the tank with water. Make sure the water surface is no longer visible from outside. If you have not yet fitted the thermometer, you should do that now. Then close the aquarium with the light hood or cover panel. Make sure the ventilator, filter, thermostat and heating are all working properly and check the temperature now and again. Once the tank has reached the right

Thermometer

Heating element

temperature, leave the water to stand for two or three days. Sometimes it takes a few days before the water has reached an even temperature but that is not a problem at all. This gives the plants a good chance to establish themselves before the fish arrive, and the water has the chance to become clear again.

Populating your aquarium

Once the temperature is right, wait a further week before you let the fish loose in the tank to prevent your fish becoming stressed with all the possible disastrous consequences. A freshly equipped aquarium contains a lot of undesirable bacteria that want to establish themselves there. You can avoid this by introducing 'good' bacteria, which will quickly take the upper hand, especially if they're supported by a properly functioning filter.

Buying goldfish

The best place to buy goldfish is a good pet shop. Don't go in on impulse. Visit the shop several times to make sure that it is always well looked after. You can also see whether the personnel pay proper attention to the aquariums.

Check that there are not always dead or half-eaten fish drifting in the tanks. An aquarium club in your area can of course give you information about good shops to buy goldfish. Once you've picked the shop, you now need to pick the fish.

Never buy fish that:
• are sick or damaged;
• are constantly snapping for air at the surface;
• swim around the floor of the aquarium in a slanted position;
• have damaged fins;
• display mould growth around the mouth;

Top: Goldfish
Bottom: Sarasa

- do not have a streamlined body form, but a hollow, ball-shaped body or one full of 'bulges';
- are constantly being chased by other fish.

It is very easy to have the 'wrong' fish imposed on you, after all you're just a beginner. Always ask for clear answers in the shop, or take someone with you that 'knows the ropes'.

Some important tips

Never put fish into a newly set-up aquarium, because it is not yet biologically in balance. All those ammoniac-destroying bacteria are not yet ready for battle. The water temperature is not yet at the right level; the tapwater still contains various chemicals, such as chloride and fluoride, which can be dangerous for our fish. Incidentally, you can quickly clear your aquarium of chloride by dissolving a few drops of chlorine in it. Your fish are highly stressed by having been caught and transported and it certainly won't help them to be set free in an aquarium that is not yet ready to receive its residents. So, once you have prepared your aquarium and filled it with water, let it stand for at least a week before you put fish in.

The first week

- Check that the filter is working properly. A filter working properly produces a strong stream of water and the outflow

for the filter should be as close as possible to the surface.
- After you've got the filter working, switch on the heating. Set it to switch on and off at about 18°C. This doesn't always work the first time. Follow the instructions that came with it exactly.
- Put the aquarium lighting on in the morning, and switch it off again before you go to bed.
- After the filter has been cleaning the water for about 24 hours, then the chloride has very probably vanished. Now you need to put the 'good' bacteria into the aquarium. To do this, buy a handful of used gravel at the pet shop. There will be more than enough 'good' bacteria in this to populate your aquarium effectively. At the same time as the gravel, buy a healthy baby goldfish, which you put into the aquarium together with the bacteria. The baby fish will produce enough ammoniac to feed the good bacteria; in turn, these quickly form colonies.
- Don't be disappointed if you notice that your aquarium has become a little cloudy after a few days. This happens because the unwanted bacteria are trying to establish themselves in your aquarium. This is finally stopped by the introduction of the 'good' bacteria. The filter must be working continuously. Only put your goldfish in when the aquarium is totally clear.

Shubunkin

Veiltail pearl scaled

Sarasa

The goldfish and its varieties

Many varieties of goldfish have been bred over the course of time. People began to breed various shapes and colours, especially in China and Japan. They make use of sudden mutations and selectively cultivate these.

The Common Goldfish

In this chapter, you can read about the various varieties of goldfish to help you make the right choices for your own aquarium.

To cultivate different varieties, breeders select fish with deviating forms into breeding tanks. The breeders use well-proven methods to establish such new varieties and preserve them for posterity. Sudden changes in shape and colour (mutations) are common among goldfish. A doubling of the caudal or anal fin, loss of the dorsal fin or the appearance of protruding eyes are regular occurrences. If left alone, these mutations will revert to the goldfish in its original colour and shape after a few generations.

The Common Goldfish
In the previous chapters, we often spoke of 'the goldfish'. This 'common' goldfish is a pretty fish with a bright orange colouring and a metallic gloss. Its head should be wide in form. If you look at the head from front to rear, it should gradually flow into the body via the dorsal and pelvic fin to the base of the tail fin. The base of the tail should be about the same width as the snout measured just in front of the eyes. The dorsal fin should start at the highest part of the back and end at the base of the tail.

The Common Goldfish can thrive not only in an aquarium, but can also be kept in a pond. It can stand cold water better than most of the other varieties. A goldfish kept in a 40 litre aquarium and properly cared for will eventually grow to a length of 20 centimetres. Bigger aquariums give the fish more opportunity to grow and goldfish of about 20 centimetres are no exception here. In large (park) ponds, the Common Goldfish can easily grow to 30 centimetres.

The Comet Fish

This is a tough little fish, regardless of whether it's kept in an aquarium or a pond. This variety is a fast swimmer and is very similar in appearance to the Common Goldfish. However, its tail is noticeably longer.

This applies especially to its forked caudal fin, which is often as long, or even longer, as the body. It is normally a brilliant deep red in colour and possesses an orange metallic gloss. In some cases these fish have mother-of-pearl coloured scales. The Comet doesn't grow as fast as the Common Goldfish and will not get as big. In a large aquarium or a spacious pond it will grow to a maximum of some 18 centimetres, although over time there have been exceptions with fish up to 25 centimetres long. The gradual elongation of the caudal fin begins when the fish is only five centimetres long.

Comet Fish

Comet Fish or Tetsugyo

The Shubunkin

This fish originally came from Japan and dates back to the beginning of the last century. In China, this fish is known as 'Chuwen-chin'. The variegated Shubunkin has bright patterns of colour and is often named 'Calico' because of that. It has mother-of-pearl coloured scales, which make brown, yellow, red, peach, grey, orange, white and black colours possible. Shubunkins with blue colourings are the most valuable. There are two forms: the London Shubunkin and the Bristol Shubunkin. The London form, in terms of colour, is very similar to the Common Goldfish. It is somewhat smaller and seldom grows beyond 15 centimetres or so. In shape and size, the Bristol Shubunkin is similar to the London variety, but its tail has grown to a very wide, forked fin. This fin is not as long as the comet's however.

Both varieties are very sought after among fish lovers, although the Bristol wins in the popularity stakes against the London. Both these varieties, along with the others covered above, are very suitable for beginners. They are excellent swimmers and can stand an inadvertent knock or two.

The Veiltail

A very well-known Veiltail is the Ryukin, which originated from Japan. This variety's back is curved very high. The Ryukin has twin caudal fins that can become as long as 15 centimetres and it otherwise has a "wide" look. This Veiltail is found in red, orange, black and white, with two-colour and sometimes three-colour markings.

These goldfish have a short, more or less egg-shaped and certainly not flat body. Looking at the head from above and from one side to the other, it is solidly built and very wide. It's difficult to tell precisely where the head ends and the body begins. Some varieties have a dorsal fin, others not. Good fish have a high, stiff dorsal fin, which is normally spherical

Veiltail 'red-black'

along the top edge. So it's not 'hollow' as in the case of 'flat' bodied goldfish. The back of those fish without a dorsal fin should be smooth, without "lumps" and indentations.

The Japanese Goldfish or Wakin

Experts believe that this goldfish was originally bred in Japan where it became known as the Wakin. This variety is characterised by the fact that it has twin tails and an oval body. Apart from this 'twin' tail it is very similar to the Common Goldfish in appearance. The overall impression is of a fantail, with the exception that all its fins appear very delicate. The long dorsal fin is carried vertically and has a rounded outer edge. There remains some space between the caudal and dorsal fins. This exceptionally graceful fish can grow to 18 cm in length, of which 10 centimetres is the tail. The variety is found with three different types of scale, so it goes without saying that it can be in a wide variety of colours. The Wakin is one of the most elegant goldfish but, sadly, also one of the most sensitive. This is because of the shape of its air-bladder, which reacts badly to very cold water. The fine tail and body fins are also easily damaged because of

Veiltail 'Calico'

their structure; rocks and items with sharp edges do not belong in their aquarium. This goldfish is not very suitable for the beginner. Sometimes, a Veiltail will be crossed with a Wakin. This produces a variety with the Japanese name 'Watonai': a Veiltail with a single tail.
This fish is very unpopular and real breeders want nothing to do with it.

The Telescope Fish (Demekin)

This remarkable variety has large eyes that look almost as if they've been mounted on an ice-cream cone. The eyes of an adult fish often stand 20 millimetres from the head. One assumes that this fish originated in China and was bred there in the 19th century. In China this fish is called 'Dragon-eye' or 'Dragon Fish'.

Japan was also very interested in this variety and at the beginning of the 20th century, there were many breeders of the Telescope in Japan, where it is known as the Demekin. Apart from its strange eye structure this fish is almost identical to the veiltail. It is never bigger than approximately 20 centimetres. It is indeed ironic that this fish, with all that eye equipment, has very poor eyesight. For this reason, you can't keep it with a lot of other fish because it has trouble finding its food. In a tank full of goldfish,

Moor

the other types will snap the food away before the Telescope Fish's very eyes. The Telescope Fish must be kept together with similar varieties with eye 'specialities'.

There is also a real 'problem fish' among the Telescope Fish. This is the descendent of a cross of veiltail and Telescope Fish or vice versa (when defining a cross, the male is always named first; thus in this case the Veiltail was the male, and the Telescope Fish the female). The babies of such a cross are generally weak and die quickly. This is a variety for experienced breeders only.

The Celestial

This fascinating variety thanks its eyes for its name. These are pointed upwards towards the sky. This fish was bred by the Chinese who gave it the name 'Ch'aot'ienyen'. This means 'the dragon that looks to the sky'. The English name is 'Celestial', which means 'seen in the sky'. There are certain advantages with this eye position: all the insects and other treats such as plant particles that swim by above are quickly detected and consumed. The eye structure is immobile; they can not look down or turn from right to left.

You'll get more pleasure from these fish if you keep five Celestials together, without other fish. Most of these fish have no

dorsal fin and are pinkish in colour, but metallic-coloured and variegated varieties have also been bred. There is even a very strange black form, which is known in Japan under the name of 'Demeranchu'. Celestials are fish for the advanced enthusiast. They are also very expensive.

Pearl scaled

The Moor

This variety is very similar in appearance to the Telescope Fish, except that it is velvety black in colour and its eyes do not stand out so far from its head. The telescope eyes are in the normal 'goldfish position', although there are fish whose eyes stand pointed straight ahead or downwards. This fish is quite sturdy and, perhaps for this reason, is often kept in garden ponds. Many goldfish beginners are interested in the Moor, perhaps because the black colour is 'in'. However, the Moor's eyes are also very vulnerable, so its aquarium must be clear of any sharp rocks or edges. As the Moor gets older, its deep black colour very gradually attains a bronze-like tint.

The Water Bubble Eye

The Water Bubble Eye is very well known. The fish thanks the unusual form of its eye for its name. This looks like a blown-up bubble. The variety is still bred at full speed in the Chinese province of Kwangtung where it is much in demand, but it remains a bizarre

Bubble Eye

Veiltail 'redcap'

fish with large 'ramparts' under the eyes. Furthermore, it has no dorsal fin. One part of the eye (the 'balloon') is filled with a gelatinous fluid. The actual eye itself is pointed upwards, although not as markedly as that of the Telescope Fish. The balloon is actually the swollen bottom eye-lid. These balloons start to develop when the fish is some six to nine months old, and by the time the fish is two years or so older, these balloons can be very big. It is then practically impossible for the fish to swim properly. It will be obvious that an aquarium with bubble eyes must not contain any rocks with points or sharp edges, because the balloons can very easily burst, and they will only grow back very slowly, if at all. This makes the fish extremely vulnerable to infections. We recommend you to only keep these fish in your aquarium when you've become a little more expert in your hobby.

Furthermore, you should not combine these fish with other fish species or goldfish varieties, but only with other Bubble Eyes. That does not need to be boring, because the Bubble Eye has been bred in many different colours, both in metallic and mother-of-pearl.

The Oranda

This splendid, stately swimmer, though somewhat strange in appearance, is highly popular. It originated from Japan where it is always called by its full name, Oranda shishigashiri, and suits the advanced fish-lover. The Oranda was first bred in 1840 and is very similar to the Veiltail. The major difference is the protuberance that is generally found on its head, and is also called the 'hood'. The hood must not cover the whole face and should be along the side of the head at most. These fleshy growths look like small bunches of grapes and start to develop when the fish is 2 to 2.5 years old. Touching the hood, it feels very soft, but is actually stronger than you might expect and damage is rare. The fish has good eyesight and can easily avoid obstacles. But the hood does have some disadvantages. Bacteria, mould and dirt can easily settle in the folds, with a risk of infection. Clean water at just the right temperature is extremely important.

The Oranda is often found in metallic gloss, with base colours from copper-red to bright red. The cherry-red varieties are a real pleasure to behold. It is inte-resting that these splendid and particularly clear colours are already present at a very young age. There is always a cherry-red 'area' on the top and the sides of the head. This area will gradually be covered by the hood. This fish is very delicate and is also now found in a brown colour (chocolate Oranda) and in blue-white. All together, this is a fish for advanced enthusiasts. Moreover, the Oranda is definitely not cheap. It is sometimes kept as a pond fish, but because of its delicate nature needs to be brought indoors in autumn and winter and put in a spacious, well equipped aquarium.

Oranda

The Lionhead

In Japan, this popular variety is known as the 'Ranchu'. Outside Japan too, this fish, which has no dorsal fin, has been able to gain a very positive reputation. It is often kept together with other slow-swimming goldfish.

The Lionhead is fully grown in about two years, and at that time it is about 13 centimetres long. It has short fins, including twin caudal and anal fins. Apart from its mouth, nostrils and eyes, the whole head is covered by a fleshy growth, reminiscent of a small bunch of grapes. This is what this fish thanks for its name: there are people who see a lion's mane in this growth. This fish is not suitable for beginners, it is far too sensitive.

Veiltail Lionhead pearl scaled

Breeding goldfish

Once you've got some experience in keeping goldfish, you can move on to the next stage in your hobby: breeding goldfish. This chapter looks at the reproductive biology of the goldfish. It would be going too far to look at the breeding of the different varieties and mutations.

The points in this chapter that apply to aquarium goldfish also apply broadly to pond fish.

Gender differences

It is almost impossible to tell the gender of young goldfish. Outside the breeding season, it is very difficult or practically impossible to tell the difference with even fully-grown fish. The best method is to buy approximately six young goldfish which you keep as breeding fish; the chance is pretty good that you'll have at least one of a different sex. When fish are fully grown, you can only tell the difference between the sexes during the spring. The females swim around with fat bellies full of eggs. On goldfish with egg-shaped bodies, the easiest way to see this is by looking at the

fish from above and comparing its 'streamline' with other fish of the same variety. The males are more slender. Watch out for white 'pimples' on the head and gills during early spring, just before the breeding season. Fish that have these pimples are without doubt males. After the males have fertilised the eggs (roe) with their 'milt', these pimples disappear. During the breeding period both genders are more intensive in colour, but especially the male.

Preparation

You can get the breeding process going yourself by keeping the breeding tank water at 11°C for a few weeks and then slowly warming it up again. As the water temperature increases you also give more food than normal.

This food should also be rich in proteins, and there are various brands available in specialist shops. Live food, such as tiny worms and shrimps also need to be on the menu. If you can't provide these yourself, you can buy them in an aquarium supplies shop. It is also important that the breeding tank is tightly planted with *Myriophyllum* (Water Milfoil), because goldfish particularly like to lay their eggs on this variety's leaves.

Mating behaviour and spawning

Goldfish are not monogamous. This means they have no particular partner. Furthermore, a male goldfish will try to fertilise as many females as possible. The mating behaviour of the male is fascinating to watch. He will follow the various females around for several days. During this first phase, both sexes become brighter in colour. Then the male will pick a female that he tries to steer into the thickest vegetation. After several hours of intense chase (also called 'driving') the female will place herself between the plants to spawn. The male presses the female against the plants and both move in a circular or spiral pattern. During these movements the eggs are 'released' and the male's milt (sperm cells) is also injected into the water, directly beside the eggs. As the eggs now swirl in the water, they finally attach themselves to the plants with the help of sticky threads. The milt falls onto the eggs, penetrates them, and fertilisation is complete.

After a few minutes, the male and the female separate, but it won't take long for the male to start driving again. After two or three hours the spawning process is complete. An adult female goldfish with a well formed body can lay some 10,000 eggs per season. Once spawning is complete, the male and the female should be removed from the breeding tank. If you don't do this they will both start enthusiastically eating the freshly laid eggs.

Development of the young

Goldfish eggs look like transparent beads for the first 58 hours. The incubation period is five to seven days depending on the water temperature (21°C). At a temperature of 18°C it lasts seven to eight days. Not all the eggs will develop into young goldfish; some eggs will become overgrown with mould and look like little balls of cotton wool. It's best to remove these from the aquarium and then mix a few drops of methylene-blue into the water.

After three or four days you can already perceive the eyes and the heart-beat in the egg; the baby fish also wriggle constantly and want to escape from the egg.

The yoke, with the fish attached to it, is clearly pigmented by the fifth day, and between the fifth and seventh day the fish will find its way out of the egg. The tail emerges first. We still call fish at this stage 'larvae'. It will attach itself together with hundreds of its brothers and sisters to plants, and to glass in corners of the tank. After several hours (this can even be a day) they let go and start to really swim. They hungrily look for food. At the tenth day the yoke is as good as 'used up' and all the young fish's food reserves have vanished.

Bringing up the young

As soon as the young 'fry' start searching for food, the most critical period in their lives begins. If there's not enough food they will inevitably die. You, as breeder, will lose the most fish during this period, so make sure you feed the young well, and enough. You can buy special goldfish breeding food (in powder form) from specialist shops. 'Live' food, such as baby shrimps and microscopic worms, must not be forgotten. This is also available in specialist shops. It is often sold deep-frozen, you must definitely let it thaw completely before using it.

Goldfish larvae are almost colourless in the beginning, but they become whitish after a few weeks. At two months they are a pale yellow. Then the fish gradually turn into their true colour. When a fish is fully grown it finally displays its final 'permanent' colour.

Young goldfish in the wild

Baby goldfish quickly form a tasty treat for all kinds of predatory fish, fish-eating birds (herons, kingfishers) and water mammals (rats). Only the fastest and most clever goldfish will survive this phase. In principle, they have no natural enemies in our aquarium. If they get the proper food and the water temperature is right, they can splendidly grow to adulthood. There are known cases where goldfish have become 25 years old.

In the wild, these first phases of life (between six and twelve months) are critical. Complicated calculations have estimated the death rate at between 70 and 80%. Besides predatory fish, birds and mammals, they have other enemies.

There are freshwater polyps (*Hydra*), leeches, water-boatmen, water scorpions, backswimmers and all kinds of water beetles and dragonfly larvae. And because the rivers, streams, lakes and ponds are sadly no longer clean, bacteria and mould diseases ensure that many goldfish throw in the towel within a year.

An investigation has proven that the greatest enemy of young goldfish are the various beetles, including the Water Beetle *(Gyrinus natans)*, described as so innocent by the poet Guido Gezelle. This beetle even eats adult goldfish. There are also raiders such as the Great Diving Beetle and the Great Silver Water Beetle.

Fish ailments

One of the worst things that can happen to an aquarium is the outbreak of a disease. A goldfish that doesn't behave normally, looks an odd colour or whose fins and tail are not spread wide may be sick.

Many goldfish suffer a long time because their owner didn't realise that his fish were sick. This chapter will cover some diseases that you might encounter when keeping goldfish. We have also tried to present as many treatments as possible.

Medicines
Lesson number one in preventing disease in your aquarium is that you should not start putting in medicines too quickly. Aquarium shops have a whole world of medicines for sale that can help you get rid of a disease. But there are huge numbers of fish that have died because too drastic action was taken, and medicines weren't administered properly. If you use medicines, read the instructions carefully beforehand.

Before you start giving your fish medicines, you would do well to ask an experienced aquarium enthusiast (ask at your local aquarium club), or ask the specialist at your aquarium shop. Medicine is not the only response in many cases. Experienced fish-lovers can probably give you a lot of advice. You would be wise to follow it.

Air-bladder paralysis
A fish can suffer from paralysis of the air-bladder. It can no longer swim and will slowly sink to the bottom of the aquarium. The animal is extremely apathetic and if it does swim, then it will be in spurts. There's not a lot you can do about air-bladder paralysis, although increasing the water temperature in the early stage can sometimes deliver positive results.

White spot

White spot is probably among the best known fish diseases. White spot is a parasite that is present in many aquariums, the *Ichthyophthirius multifilis*. A healthy fish can offer it resistance, but if there's one fish in your aquarium with weakened resistance, the parasite will settle on it. Once that's happened, the parasite multiplies immediately. These offspring can then 'attack' healthy fish too and cause an explosive development of the disease. There is a medicine available in specialist shops that kills the parasite. You can also use Halamid (*benzolsulfonchloramides natricus*) in a concentration of 1:1,000,000. Sulphamezathine Sodium is also used, but difficult to find (vet or chemists). Use a 33 1/3 percent solution (3 cm^3 per 100 litres of water). If your fish has this disease, you will see irregular white spots over its whole body. They first appear on the tail and other fins. You must act fast to prevent an explosion of the disease.

White spot

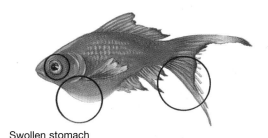

Swollen stomach

The Freshwater Louse
(*Argulus foliaceus*)

This some eight millimetre large parasite can easily come with the water fleas you may have caught for your fish in the wild. You can recognise it because of its size. It attaches itself to a fish. If you want to be rid of it you must remove the affected fish from the aquarium. Put some aquarium water in a shallow tank and put the fish in.

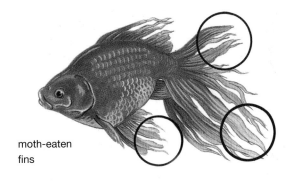

moth-eaten
fins

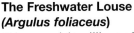

Then stroke a pencil that has been dipped in mercurochrome over the parasite. This will normally let go quickly. Don't get too close to the gills. There are possibly other treatments available in your aquarium shop.

White fuzzy fungal growth

Rust or gold disease

A fish suffering from this disease looks as if it has been strewn with pepper. Small yellow-brown spots appear, particularly on the fins. It is a parasite, *Oodinium pilularis* or *Oodinium ocellatum*. You can fight it with aureomycine (concentration of 10 mg per litre of water), also with medicinal methylene blue (1 gram per 100 cl water; of this solution you use 10 cc per 100 litres of water). Here too, there are other medicines available.

Mould

Whenever mucous membrane has been damaged for one reason or another (sharp rocks for example) mould can arise: grey or whitish threads on wounds in particular.

The fish's fins become covered. Set the fish in oxygenated old water and increase the temperature by three degrees. Using a pencil, wipe the wounds with a 10% kitchen salt solution. Here too, don't get too close to the gills.

Ichtyophonus hoferi

This parasite lives generally inside the fish's body, but occasionally may appear on the skin (recognised by a yellowish white bead). Set the patient apart in oxygenated water. Improvement is usually spontaneous, especially if you increase the temperature somewhat now and again. There are also medicines available in specialist shops.

Goldfish on the internet

A great deal of information can be found on the internet. A selection of websites with interesting details and links to other sites and pages is listed here. Sometimes pages move to another site or address. You can find more sites by using the available search engines.

www.bristol-aquarists.org.uk/index.htm
Look here for information about the different fancy goldfish varieties, how to keep them, and how to breed them.

www.goldfishsociety.org/
The goldfish society of America.

www.goldfishparadise.com/
The Goldfish Paradise Society is a global community of goldfish enthusiasts that share a common bond: their affection for goldfish and their desire to share their knowledge/experiences to further goldfish health and well-being.

www.londonaquarium.co.uk/
One of Europe's largest exhibits of aquatic life.

www.goldfishguy.com/
US site with general goldfish keeping information and pictures.

www.easyfishkeeping.com/
Fish keeping help site, includes online calculators for tank volume etc.

www.thegoldfishbowl.co.uk/
This long-established shop is one of the most famous in Britain. On this site you can find lots of information on goldfish and their care.

www.fishkeeping.co.uk/index.php
Fish retailers, vets and clubs in the UK.

Clubs

Becoming a member of a club can be very useful for good advice and interesting activities. Contact the Club in case addresses or telephone numbers have changed.

Goldfish Society of Great Britain
Ms. Christine Griffin, 23 Green Lane, Northgate, Crawley, West Sussex RH10 2JX, England.

Bristol Aquarists Society
Email: bob.jones@ntlworld.com
www.bristol-aquarists.org.uk/index.htm

Goldfish society based in the Midlands
Email: dave@tucker228.freeserve.co.uk

Goldfish society based in Sunderland
Email: B.Parkin@btinternet.com
www.castaways56.supanet.com/

The Goldfish Society of America
PO box 551373
Fort Lauderdale
FL 33355
USA
email: info@goldfishsociety.org

Profile of the Goldfish

Latin name:	*Carassius auratus*
Length:	6 to 40 cm (2 to 15 inches) depending on space and food quality
Food:	Both vegetable and animal food
Water temperature:	18 to 21°C (64 – 70°F)
Water hardness:	Maximum 6 DH
Special breeding characteristics:	Like to lay eggs on *Myriophyllum* (Milfoil)
Incubation time for young:	5 to 7 days, depending on the temperature
Life expectancy:	25 years